Europe Coloring Book!

A Unique Collection Of Coloring Pages For Kids

Bold Illustrations
COLORING BOOKS

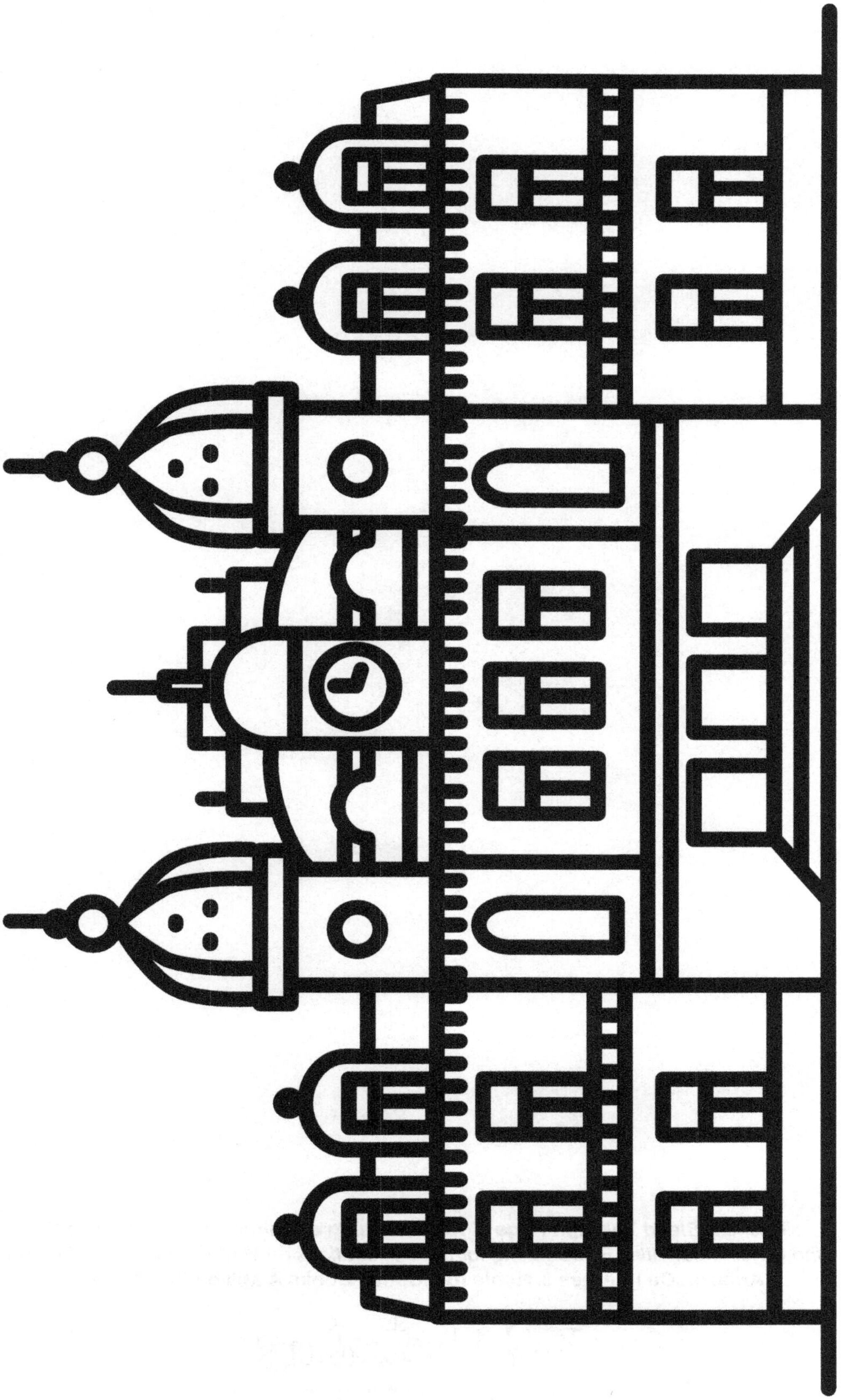

This is a Bleed Through Page If You Are Using a Colouring Marker or Pen!

Find Other Great Titles By searching for Bold Illustrations on Your Favorite Book Retailer

Amazon.Ca | Barnes & Noble (BN.Com) | Books A Million (BAM.Com)

Bold Illustrations

COLORING BOOKS

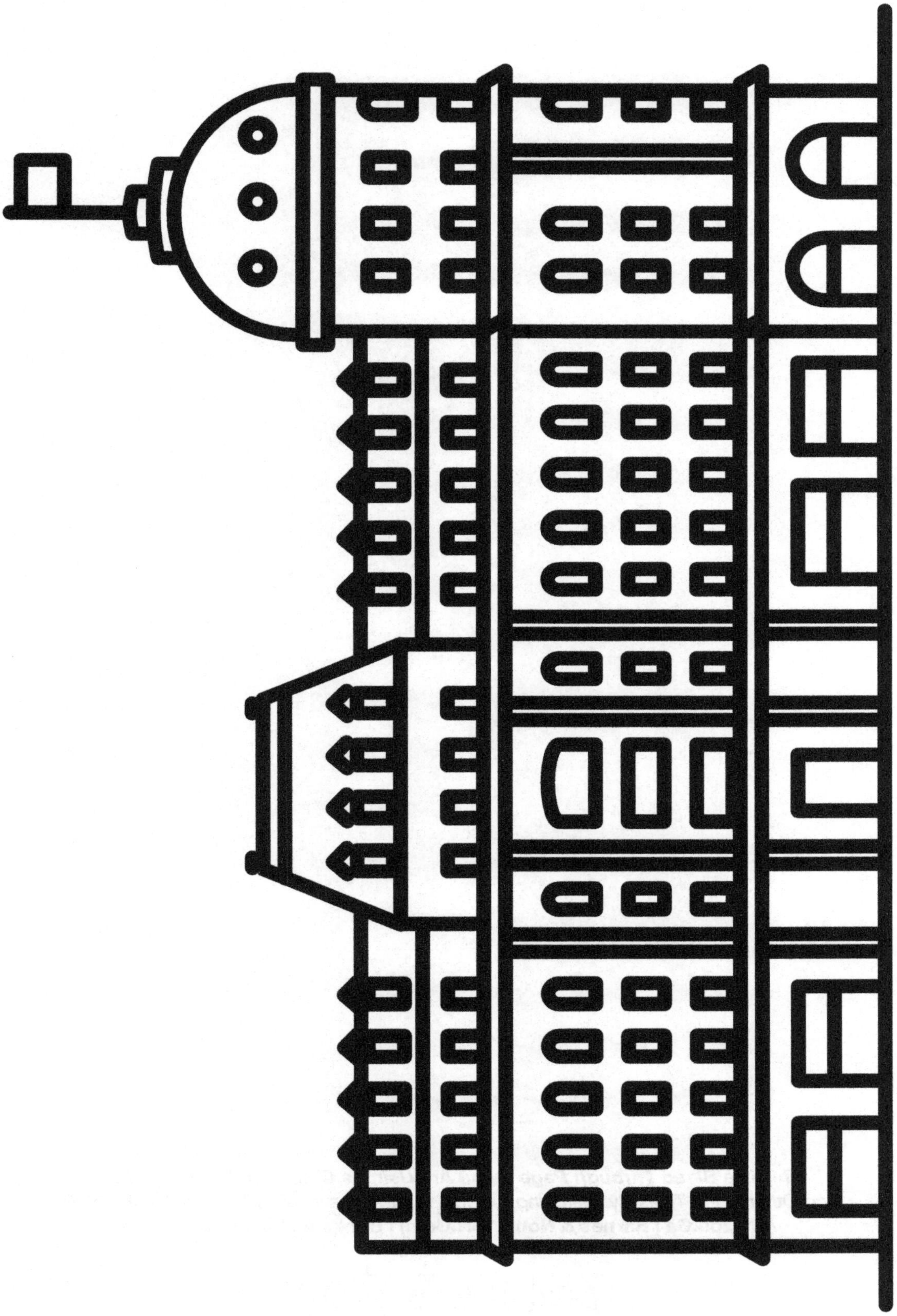

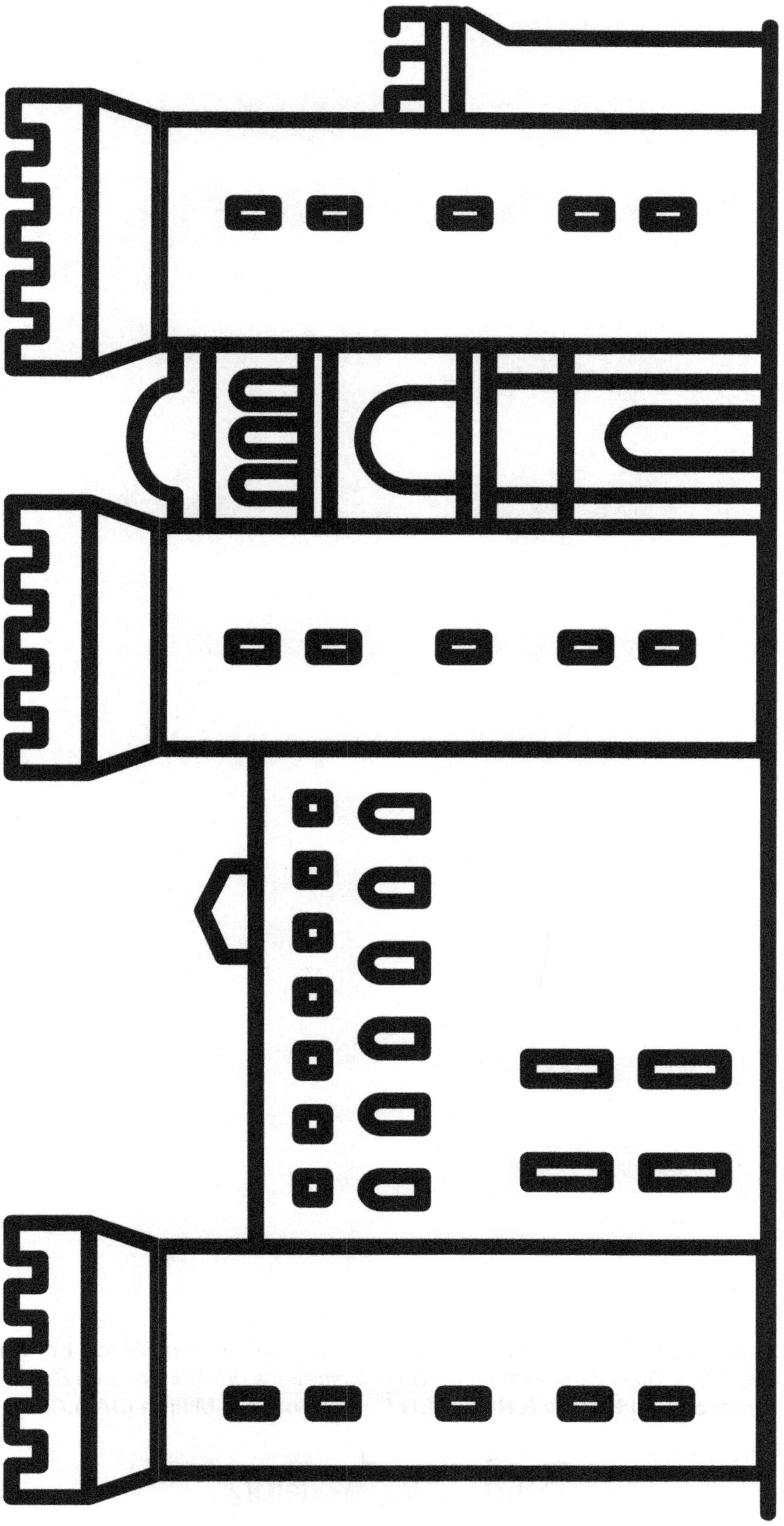

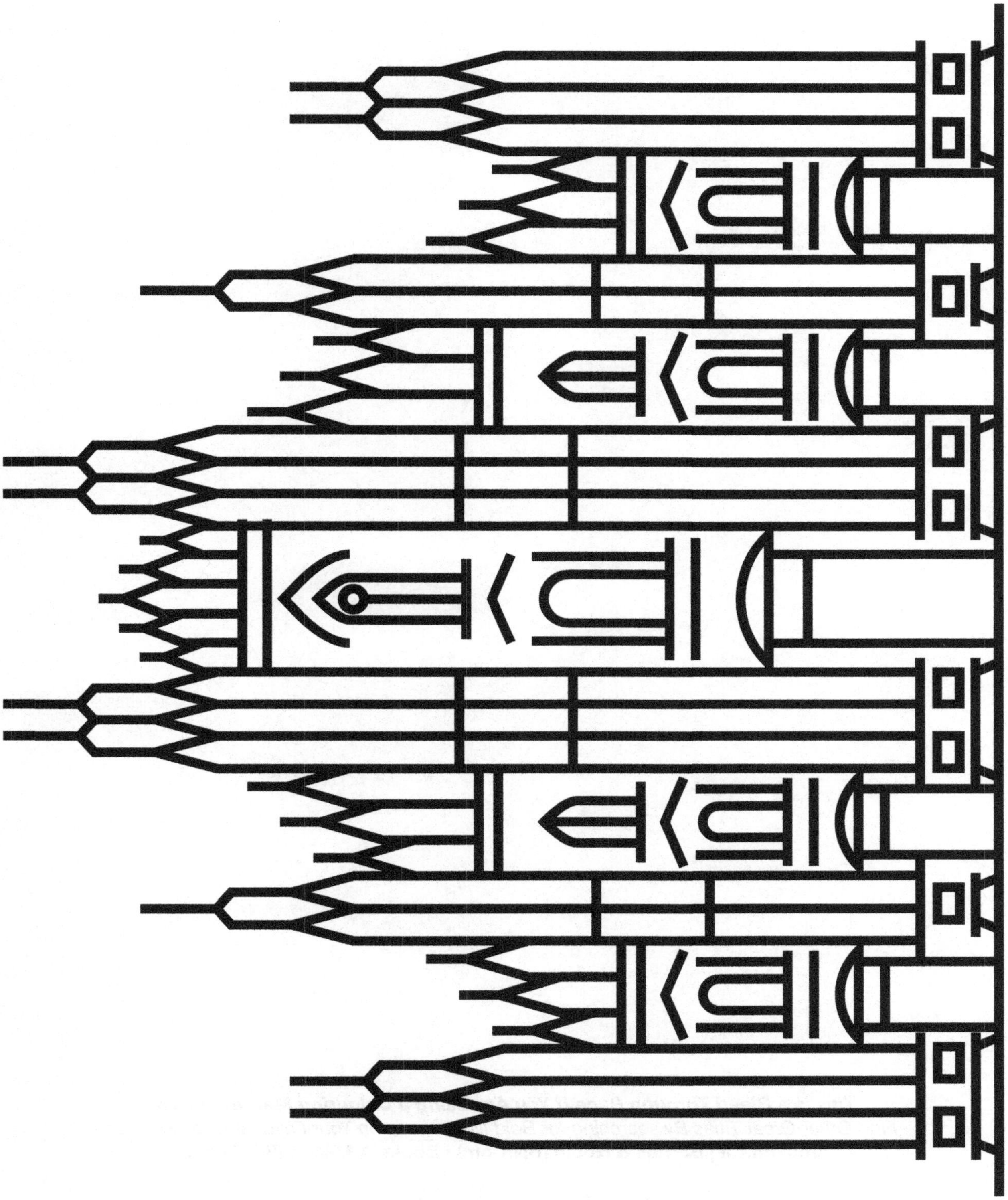

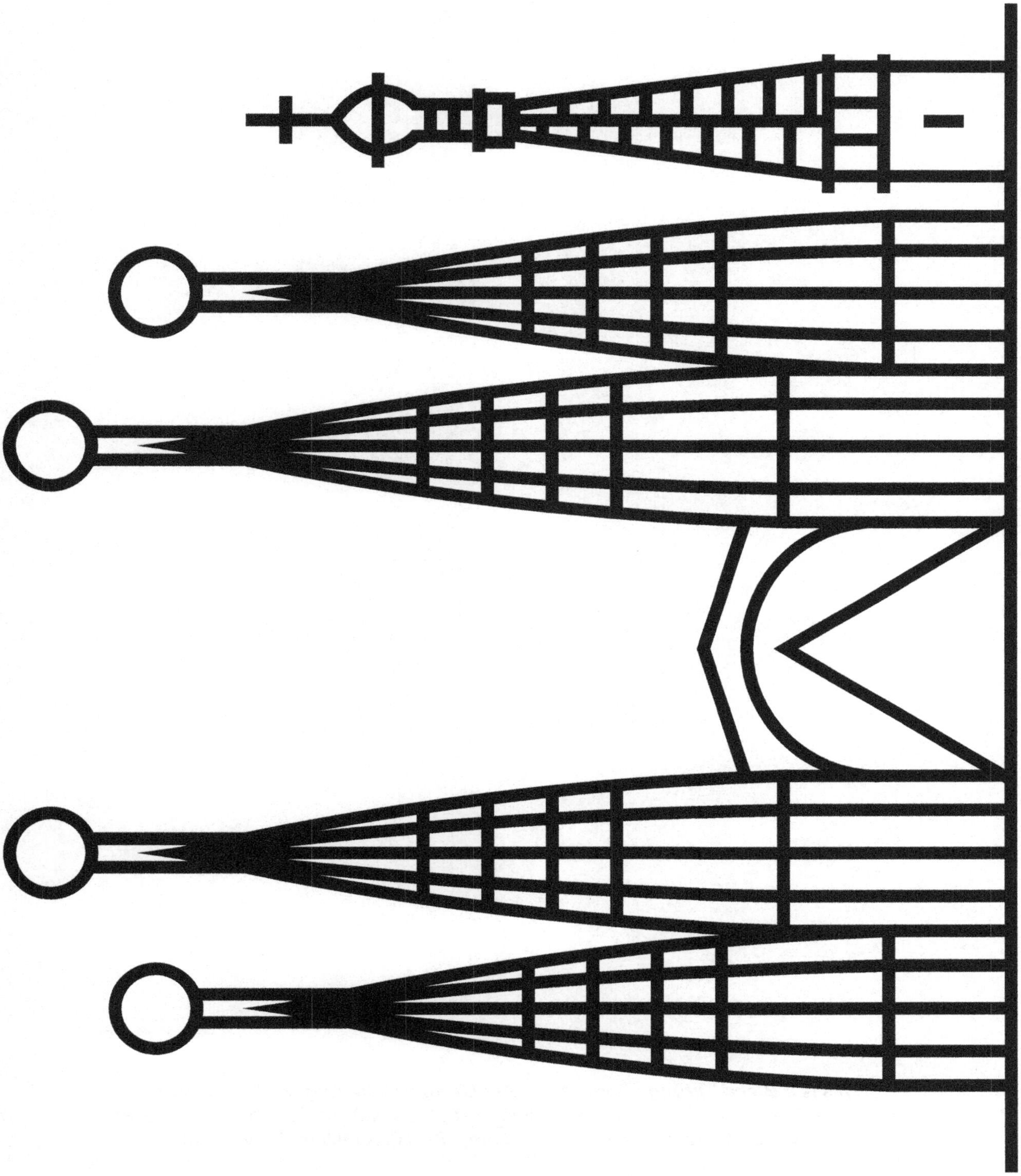

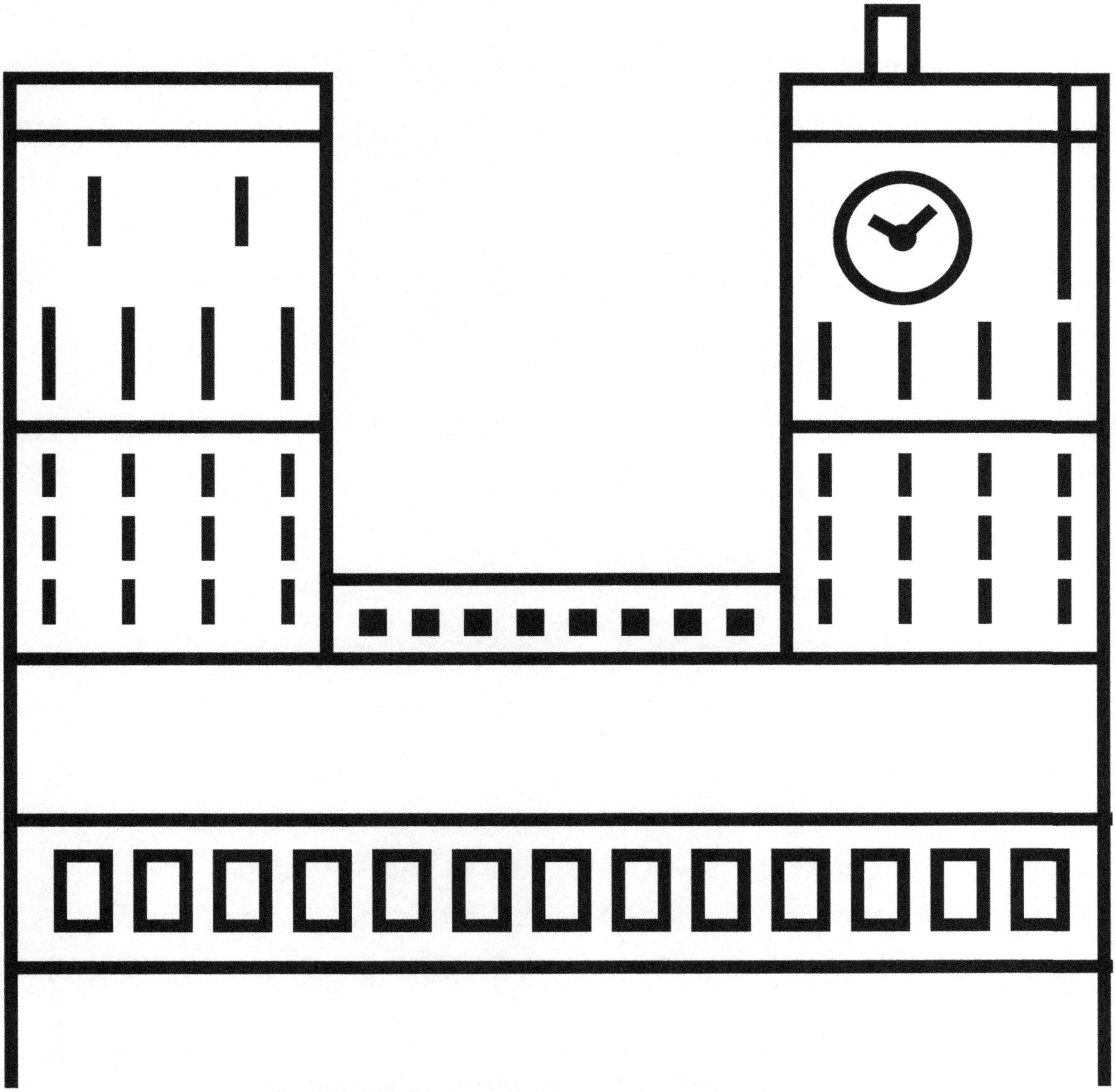

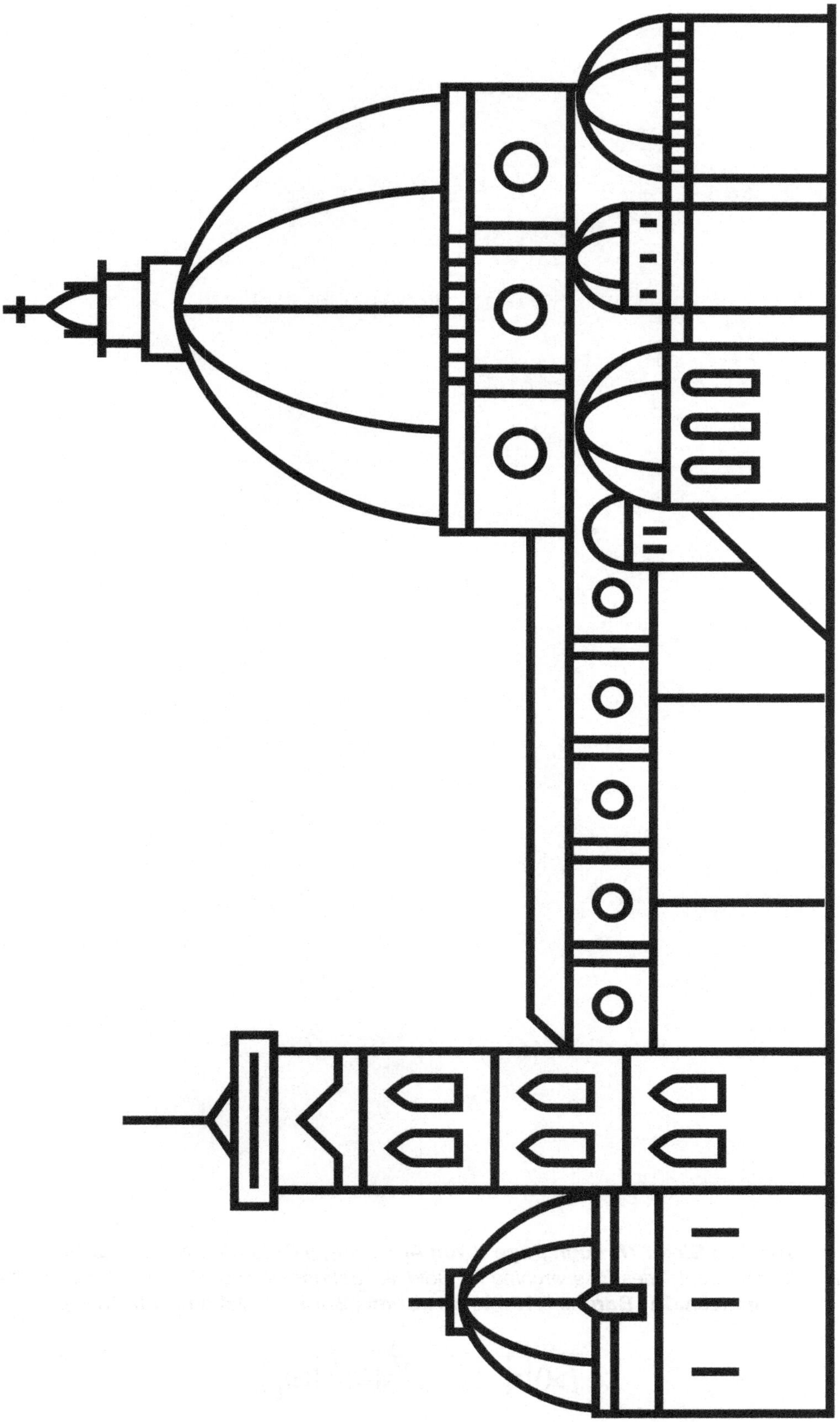

This is a Bleed Through Page If You Are Using a Colouring Marker or Pen!
Find Other Great Titles By searching for Bold Illustrations on Your Favorite Book Retailer
Amazon.Ca | Barnes & Noble (BN.Com) | Books A Million (BAM.Com)

Bold Illustrations
COLORING BOOKS

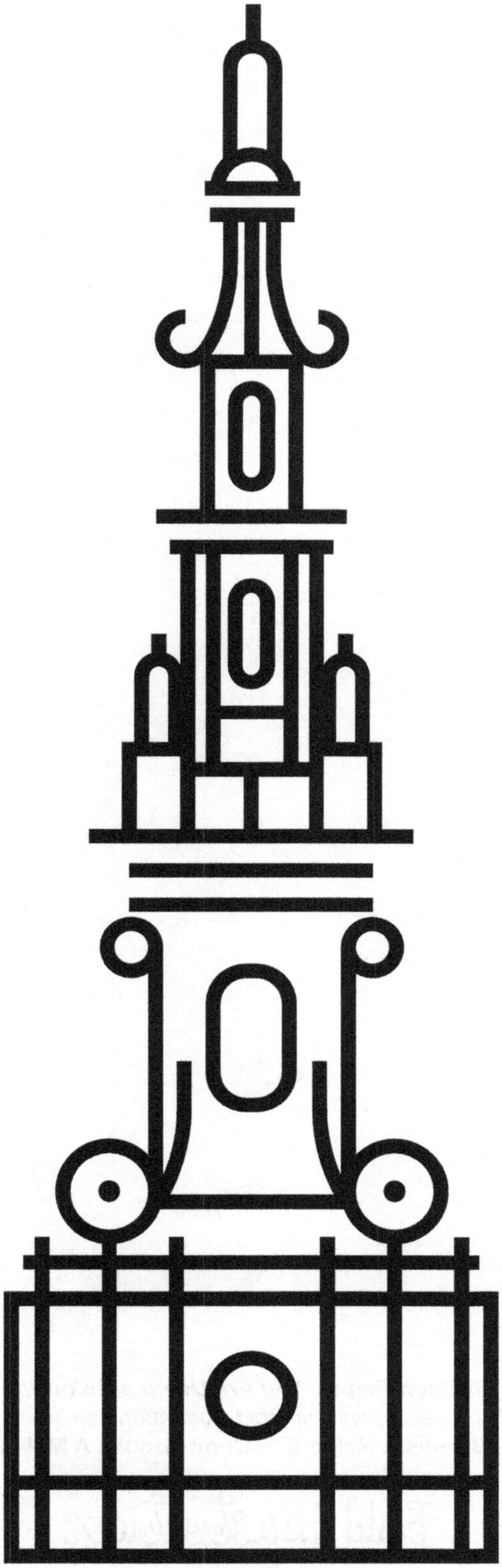

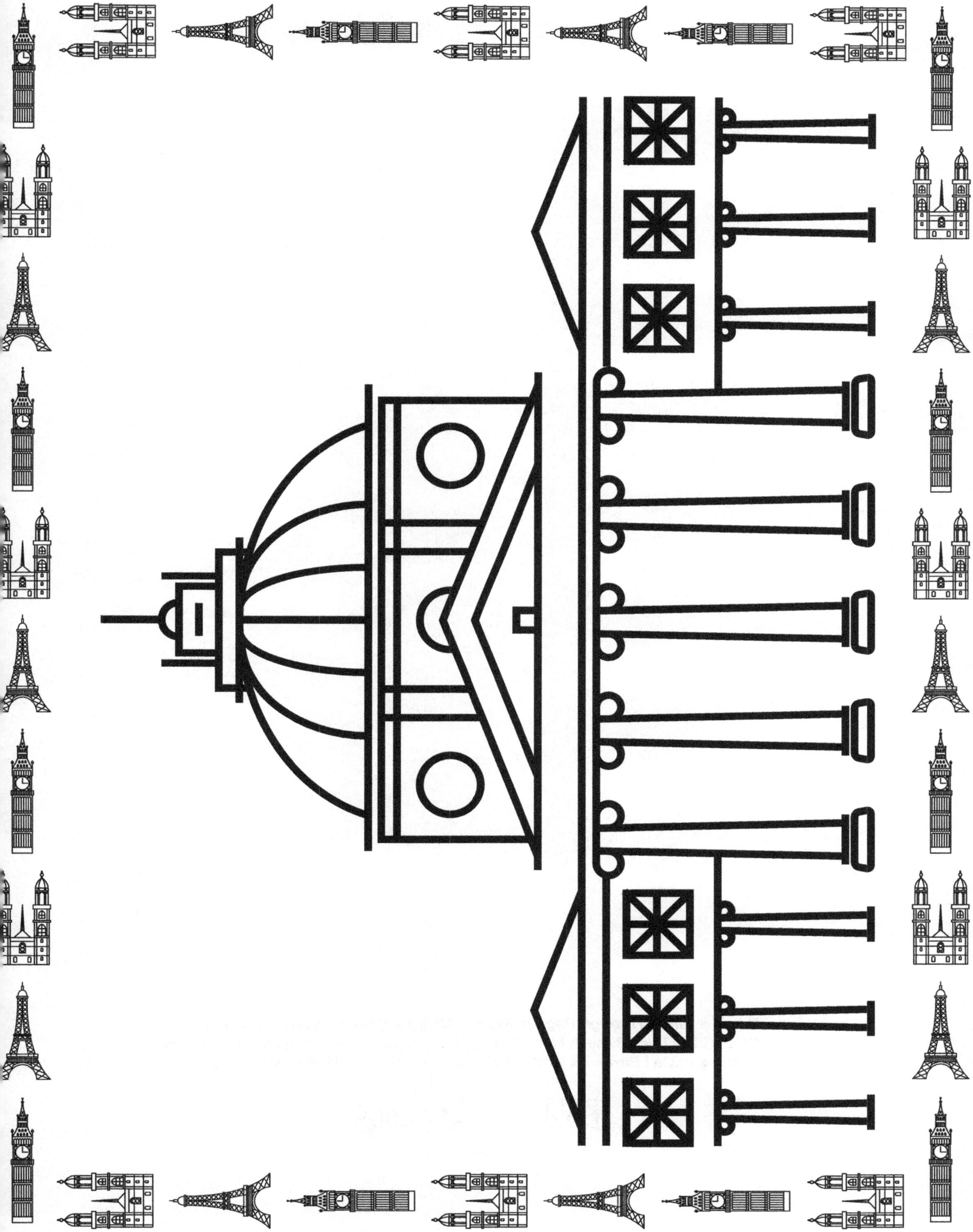

This is a Bleed Through Page If You Are Using a Colouring Marker or Pen!
Find Other Great Titles By searching for Bold Illustrations on Your Favorite Book Retailer
Amazon.Ca | Barnes & Noble (BN.Com) | Books A Million (BAM.Com)

Bold Illustrations
COLORING BOOKS

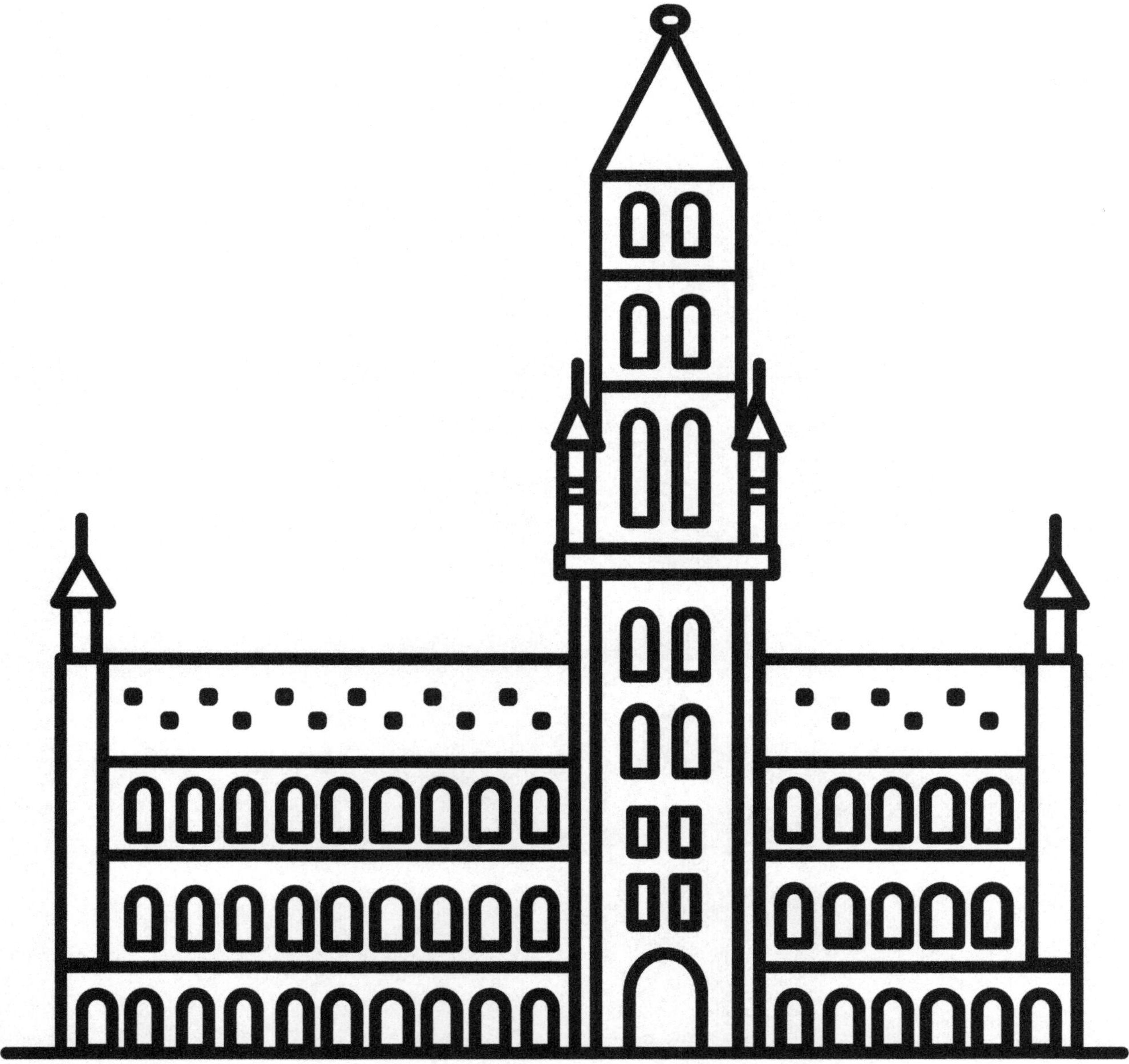

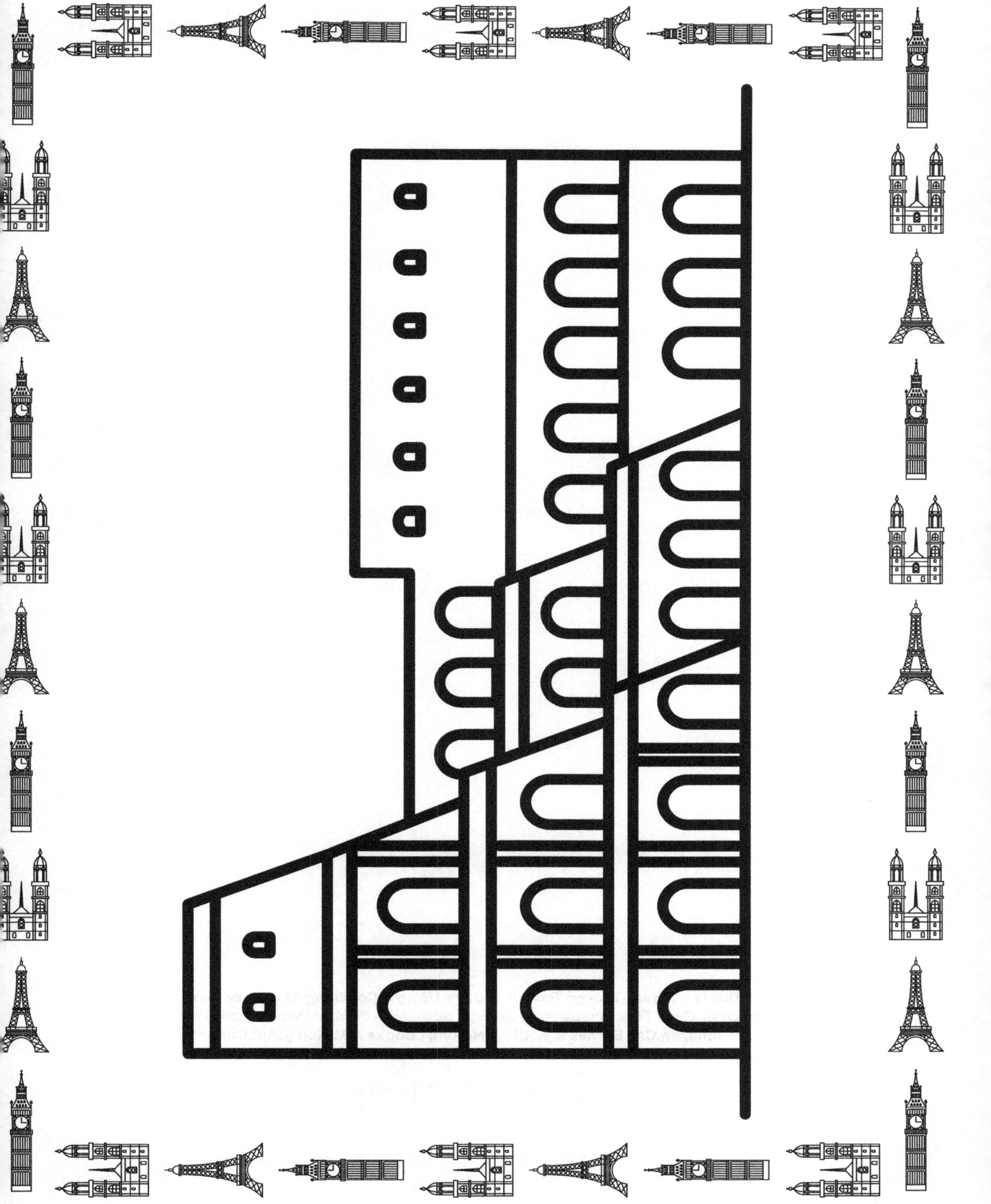

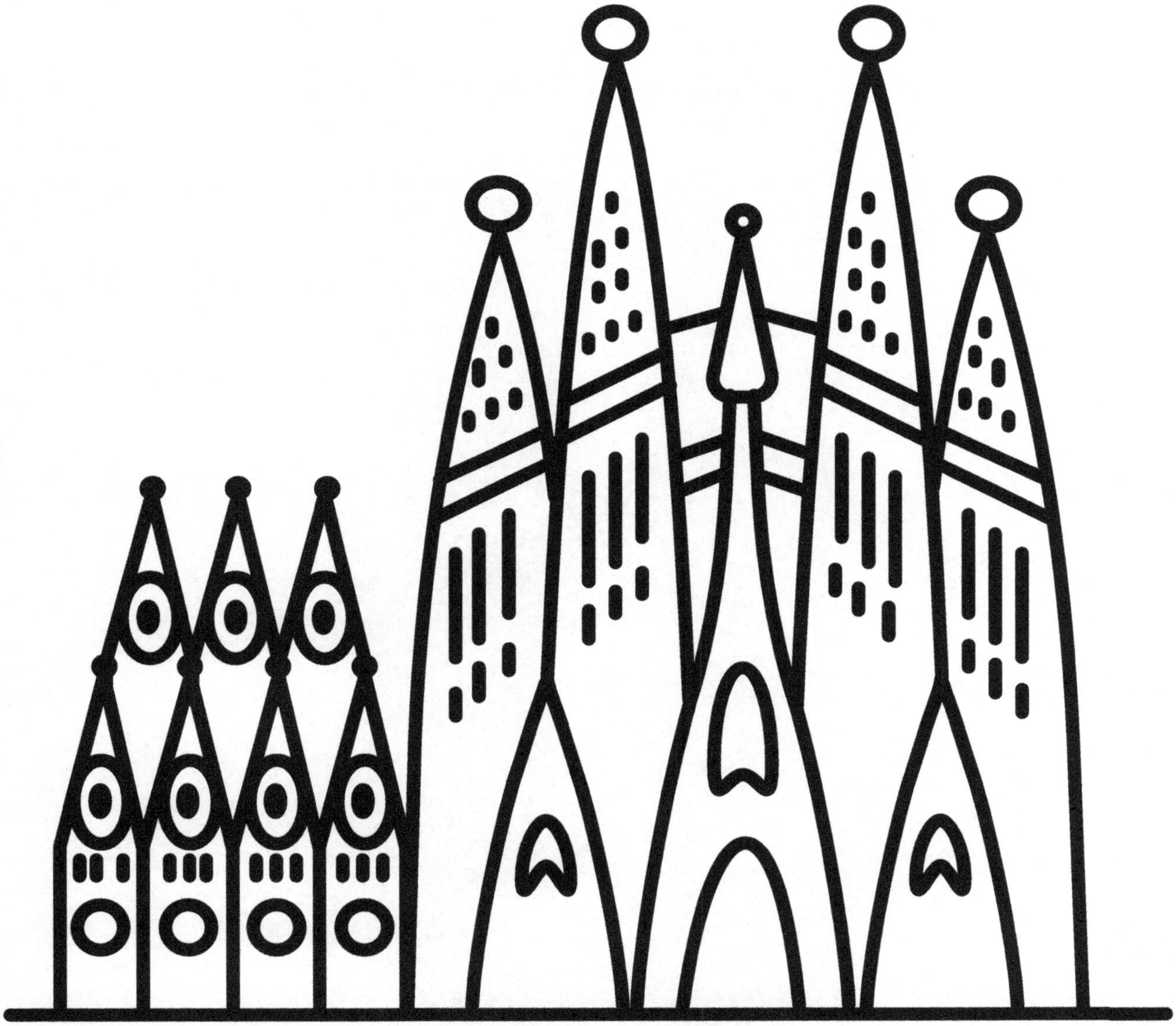

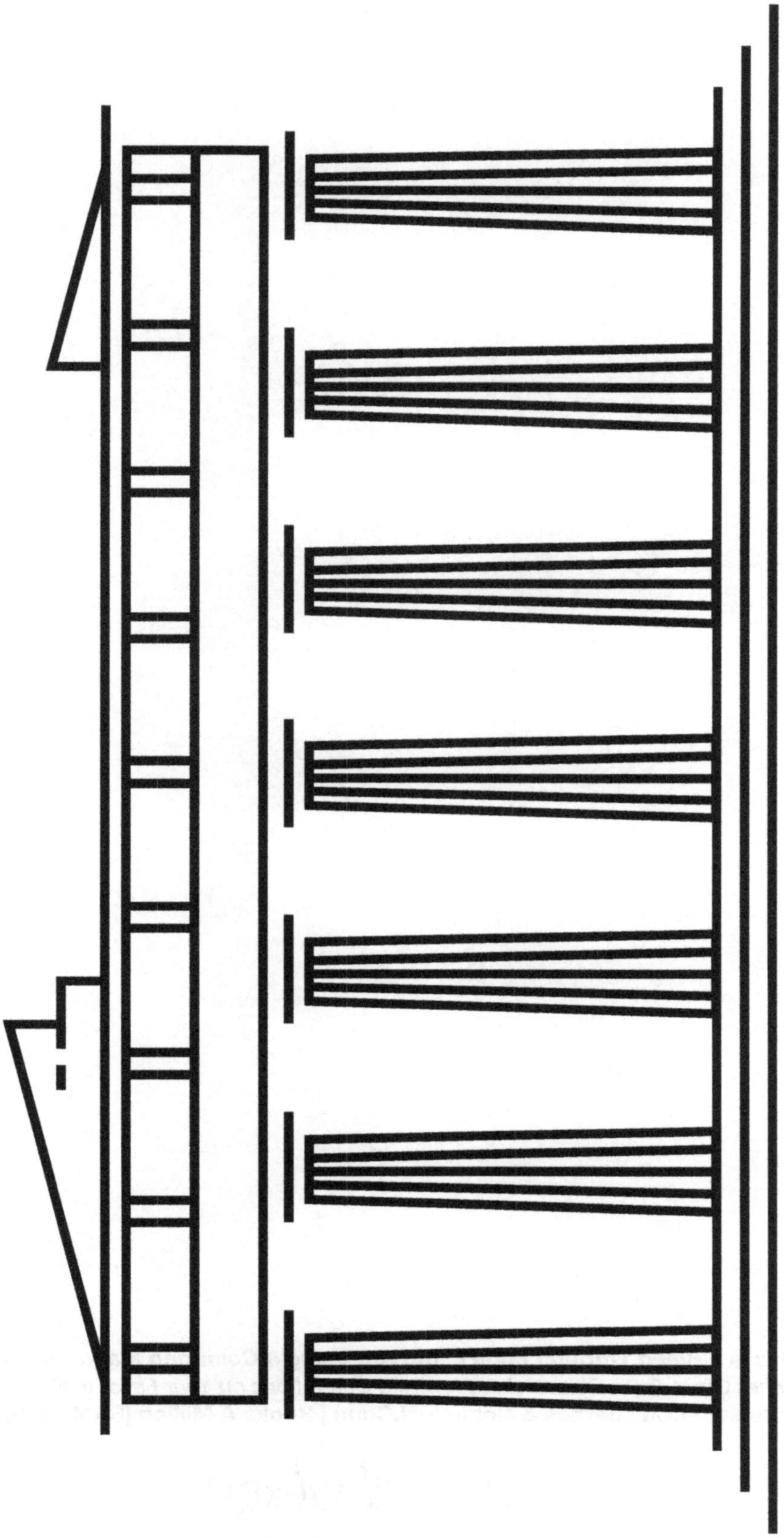

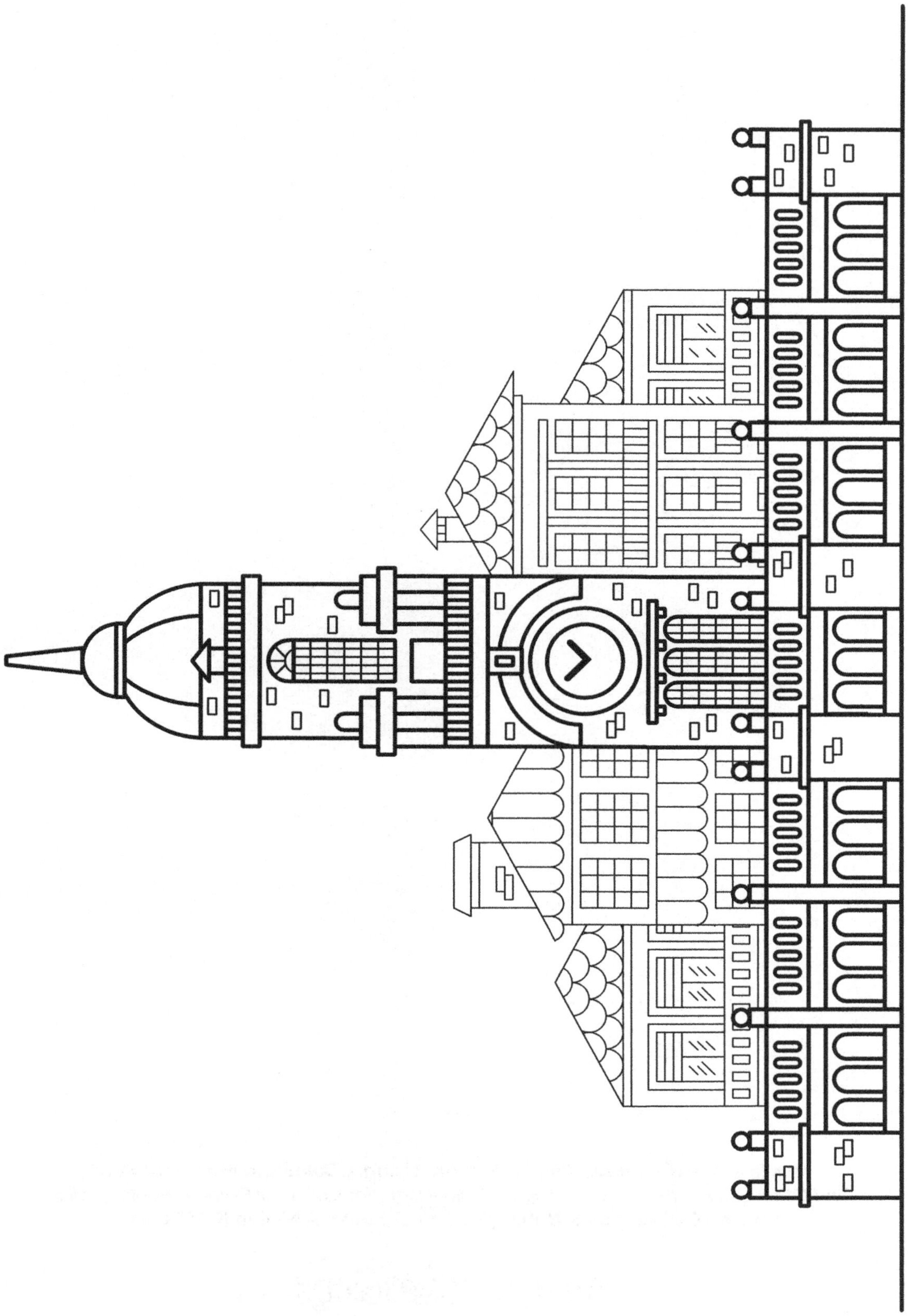

This is a Bleed Through Page If You Are Using a Colouring Marker or Pen!

Find Other Great Titles By searching for Bold Illustrations on Your Favorite Book Retailer

Amazon.Ca | Barnes & Noble (BN.Com) | Books A Million (BAM.Com)

Bold Illustrations

COLORING BOOKS

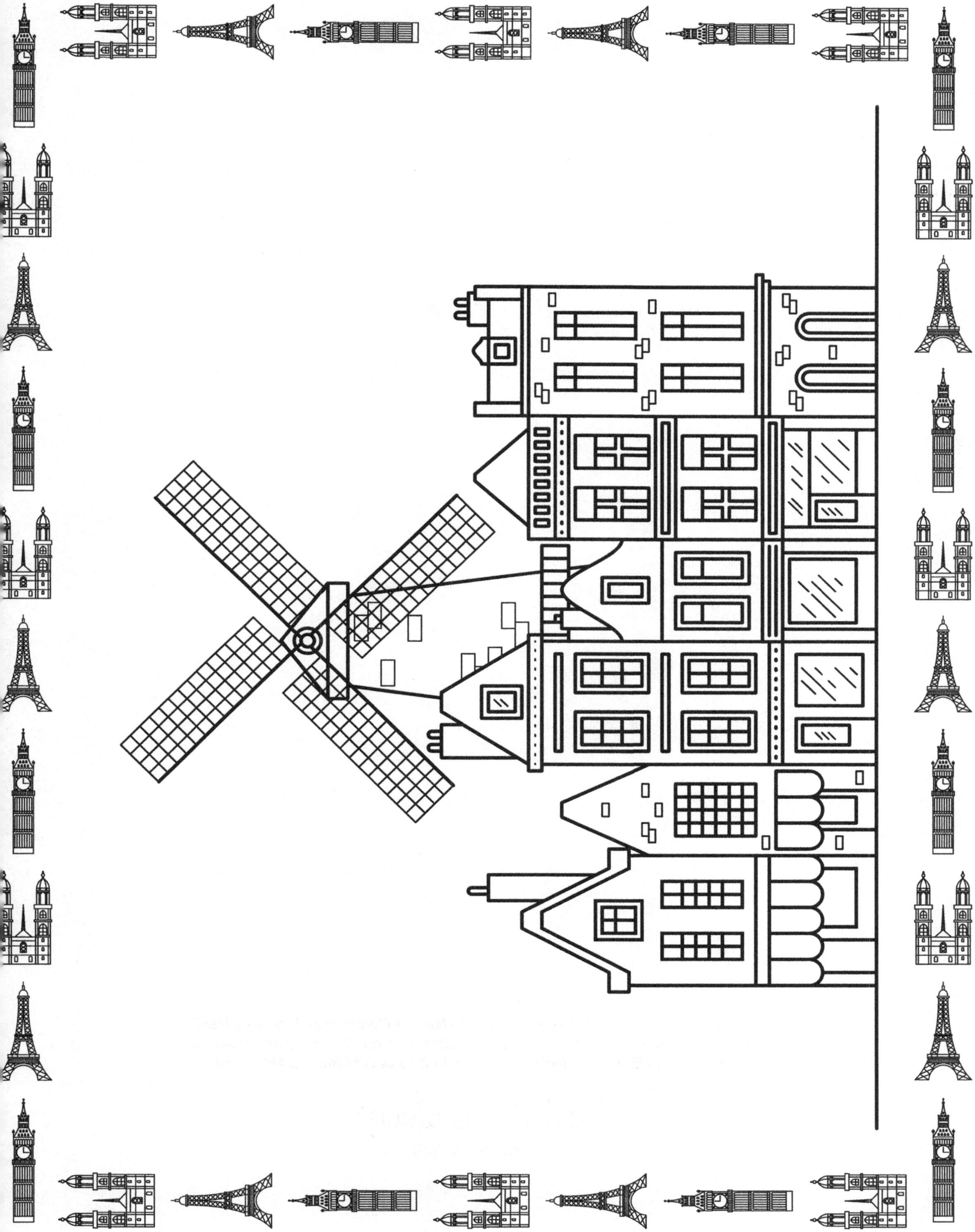

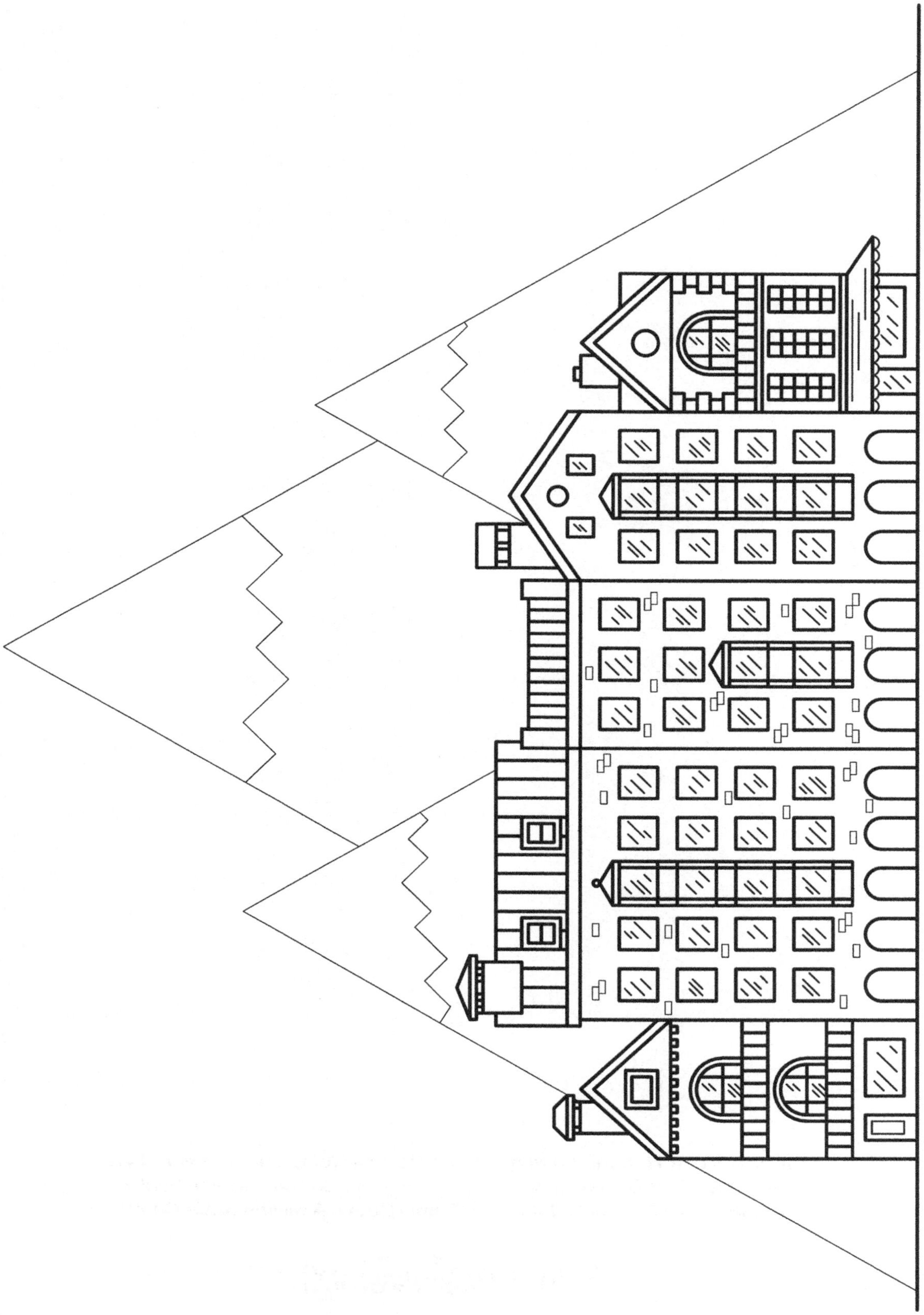

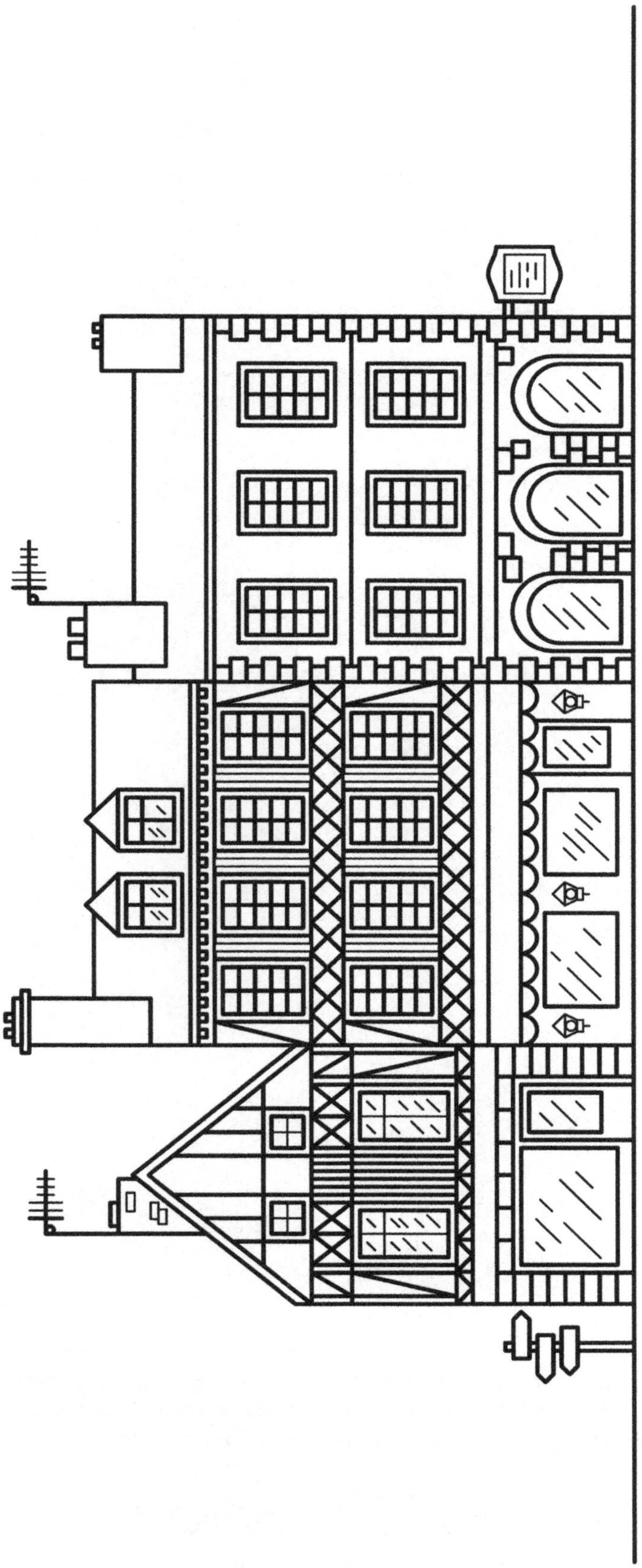

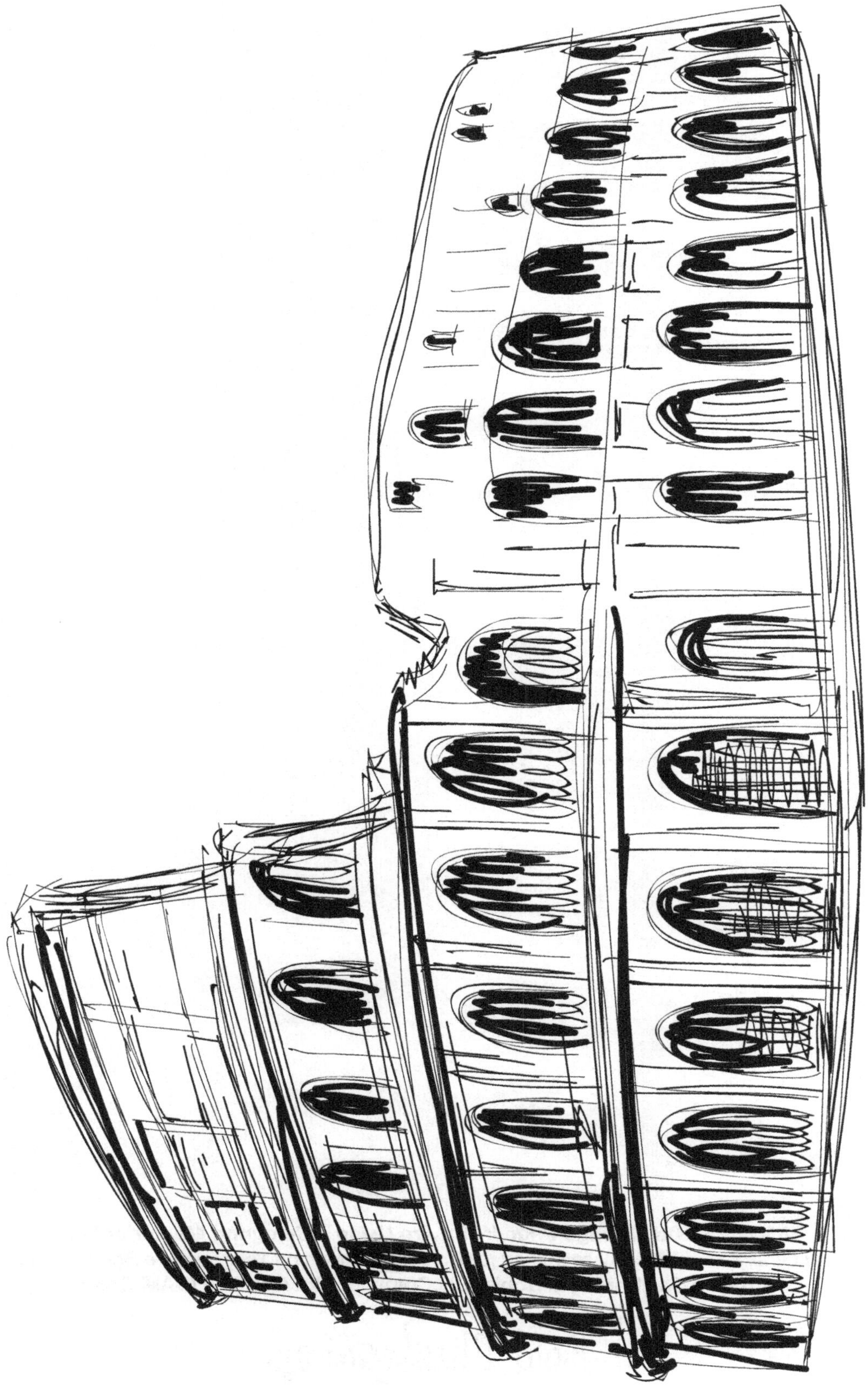

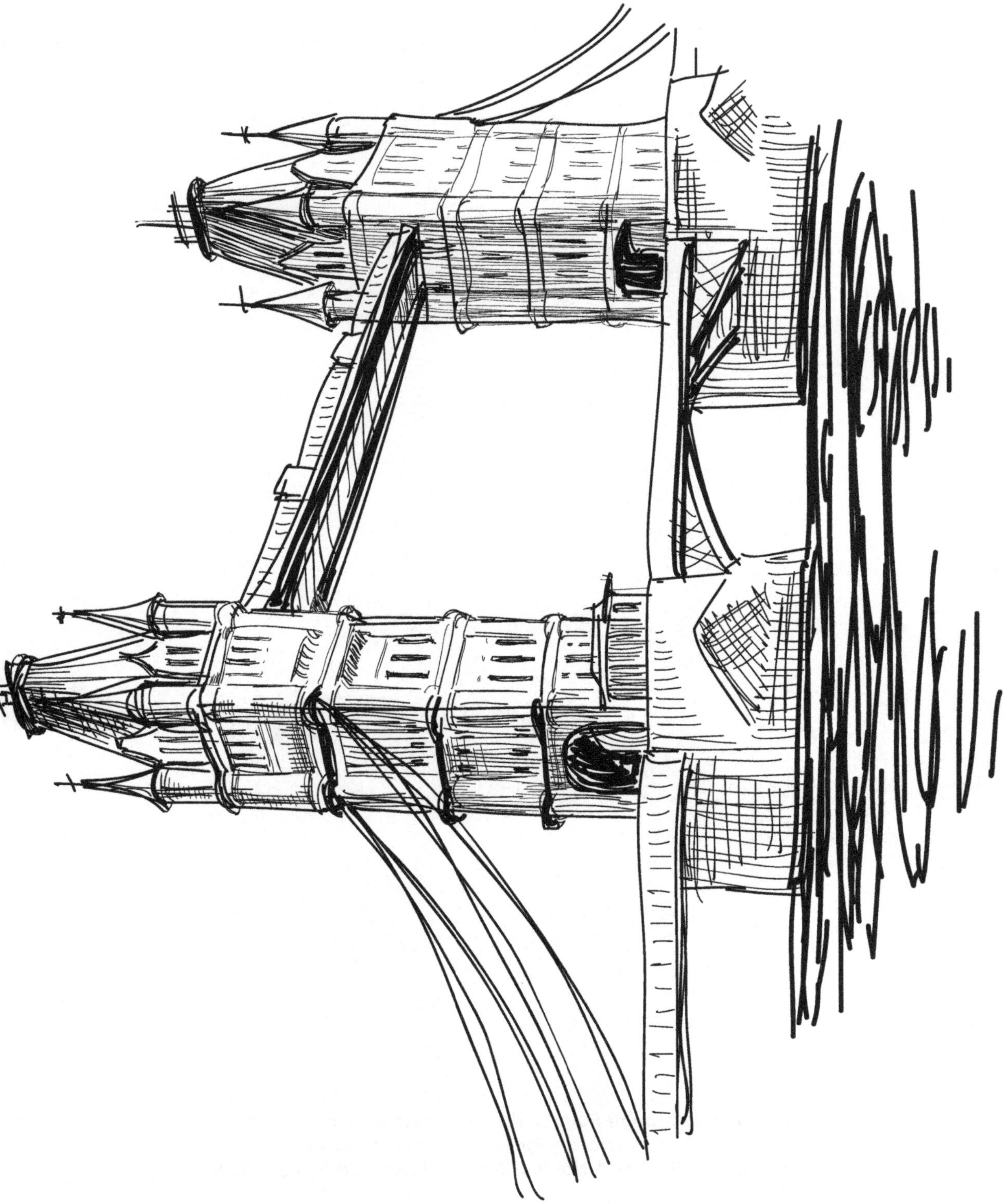

This is a Bleed Through Page If You Are Using a Colouring Marker or Pen!

Find Other Great Titles By searching for Bold Illustrations on Your Favorite Book Retailer

Amazon.Ca | Barnes & Noble (BN.Com) | Books A Million (BAM.Com)

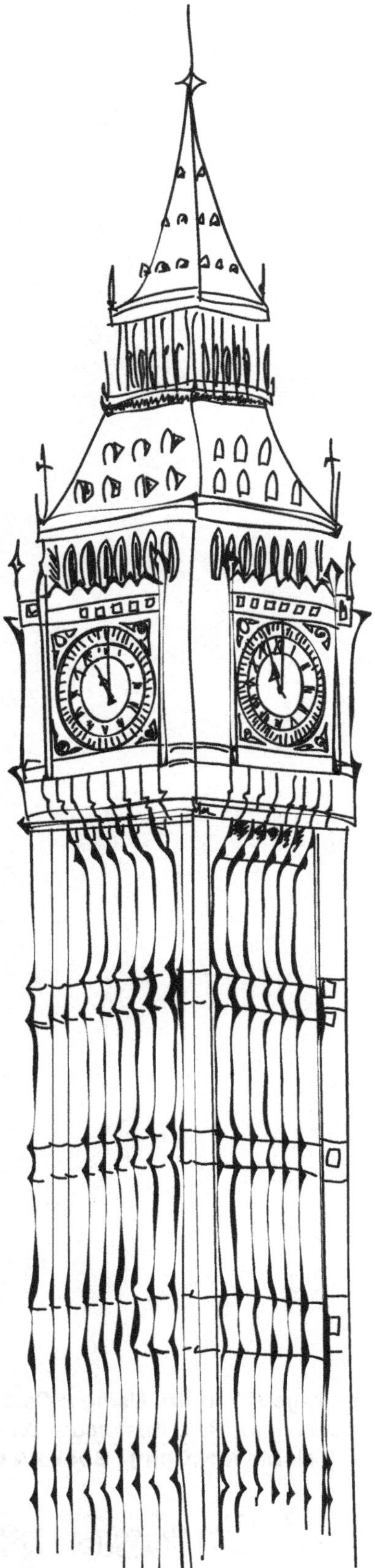

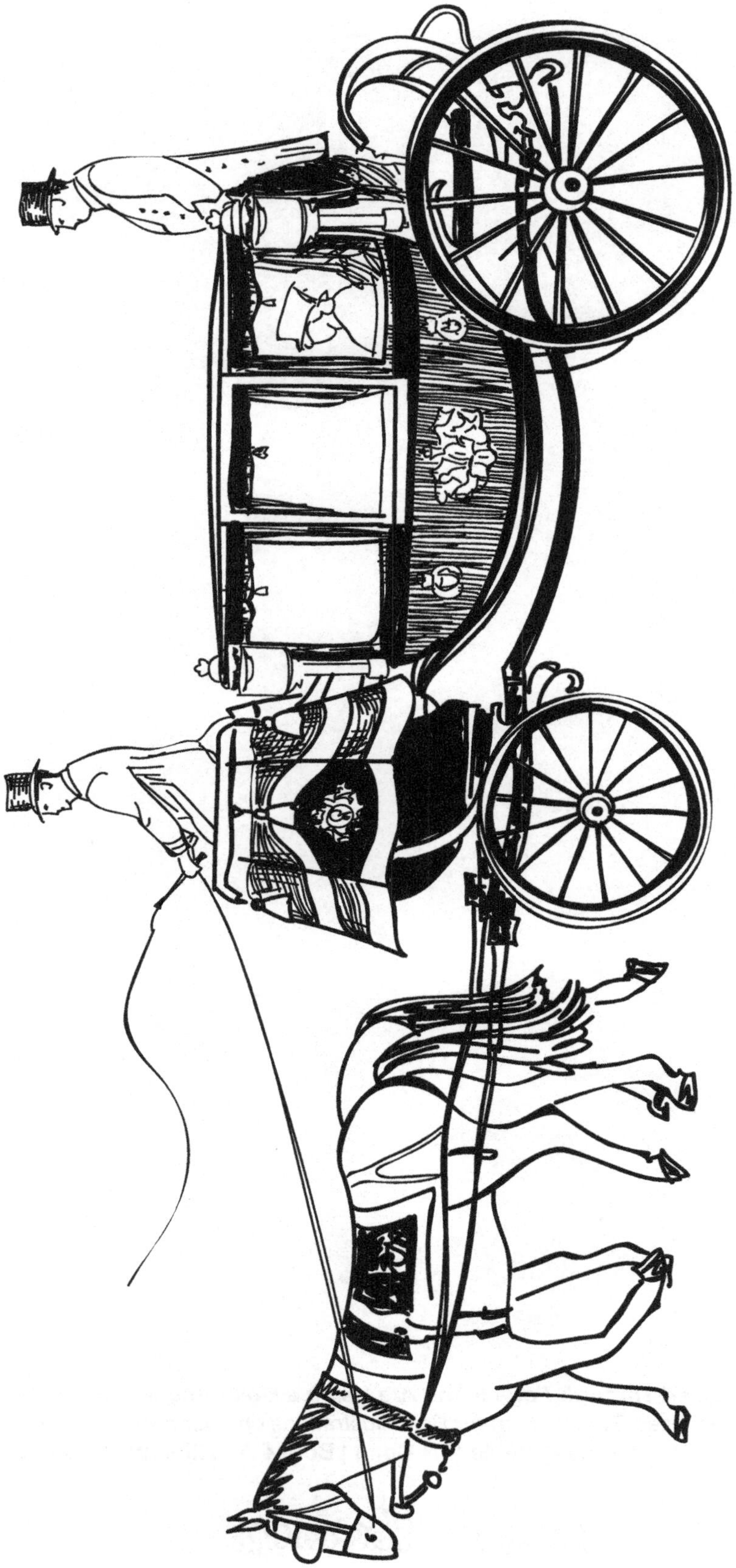

Made in the USA
Coppell, TX
05 March 2024

29798708R00046